ERNEST PORTER

FACING
ERNEST

FINDING OUR PATH TO

INNER PEACE AND FREEDOM

Ernest Porter

FACING ERNEST PORTER

Copyright © 2023

No part of this book may be reproduced in any form,

by photocopying or by any electronic or mechanical means,

including information storage or retrieval systems,

without permission in writing from both the copyright

owner and the publisher of this book.

First Published Date by

Publishers Details Here

Printed and bound in Great Britain by

www.print2demand.co.uk

Westoning

Dedication

To my dearest parents and cherished friends,

This book is not only a labor of love but a culmination of the countless moments you've believed in me, lent a shoulder to lean on, and offered unwavering encouragement. The tears and triumphs, the late nights and early mornings – you've been there through it all, standing by me with steadfast faith.

As I pen down these words, I can't help but be overwhelmed by the depth of gratitude I feel for each of you. Your love, your presence, and your unyielding support have been the backbone of my journey. Through every obstacle, you've been the guiding stars, lighting my path with your warmth and reassurance.

This book, in many ways, reflects the strength and inspiration I draw from our shared moments. It's a tribute to the bonds we've forged, the memories we've created, and the belief you've instilled in me. With every word written, it is your spirit that flows through these pages.

In your love and friendship, I've found the courage to pursue my dreams. For that, I dedicate this book to you with all the love and emotion in my heart. It's not just my book; it's our story.

Written with heartfelt appreciation and love to everyone who reads Finding Ernest, and it changes their life.

Acknowledgment

I am overwhelmed with gratitude as I pour my heart out to express my deepest appreciation. Today, I want to extend my heartfelt thanks to every single person who supported me on my first journey, "Reflections of a Soul." It is with an overflowing sense of gratitude that I reach out to each one of you.

To the podcast hosts and radio personalities who graciously opened their platforms for me to share my thoughts and experiences, I am eternally grateful.

Your willingness to give me a voice and provide a platform to spread my message means more to me than words can convey. Through your generosity, you helped me touch the hearts and souls of countless individuals, and for that, I am forever indebted to you.

But amid this overwhelming gratitude, I cannot forget the two extraordinary women who have been the very foundations of my existence.

Primarily, my dear mother, Mary Porter, a force of love and resilience. You, my beautiful mother, have shaped me into the person I am today.

Your unwavering support, your gentle guidance, and your unconditional love have molded my character and given me the strength to overcome any obstacle in my path.

Facing Ernest Porter

Thank you, Mom, for being the embodiment of love and for instilling in me the belief that I can achieve greatness.

And to my beloved wife, Lyndia Porter, words cannot express the depths of my gratitude for your unyielding support and unwavering belief in me.

You have been my anchor, my confidante, and my biggest cheerleader. Your boundless love, patience, and understanding have propelled me forward when doubt threatened to consume me.

Thank you for standing by my side, for encouraging me to follow my passion, and for sharing in every triumph and setback along the way. Thank you, my love, for being my rock, sanctuary, and inspiration.

To my beloved children who have shown me kindness, love, and support, please accept my heartfelt thanks. Your encouragement and belief in me have touched my soul in ways that words alone cannot describe.

Your presence in my life has made a world of difference, and I will forever cherish the impact you have had on my journey.

As I reflect upon this incredible chapter of my life, a calm sense of peace and joy settled upon me that filled my mind with a sense of awe and profound gratitude. Thank you for believing in me and for allowing me to share my story.

# Contents

Dedication iii

Acknowledgment iv

Preface vii

Introduction xii

Chapter 1 The Awakening 1

Chapter 2 Embracing Your Worth 19

Chapter 3 Grateful Reflection Journey 27

Chapter 4 Unravelling Self-Hatred 32

Chapter 5 Reflections of Change 42

Chapter 6 Mirror of Self-Discovery 48

Chapter 7 Writing My Story 57

Chapter 8 Embracing Self Discovery 66

About The Author 74

Preface

"Facing Ernest has been a transformative experience that has expanded my horizons and challenged my preconceived notions. It has compelled me to venture beyond the confines of my comfort zone and explore the depths of my being.

Through this journey, I have come face to face with my strengths, weaknesses, desires, and fears, unearthing a tapestry of emotions that have long been suppressed.

In a world driven by instant gratification and the pursuit of external validation, 'ME' has served as a beacon of authenticity and self-discovery. It has forced me to confront the masks I wear and the roles I play, encouraging me to peel back the layers and embrace the rawness of my true self.

This process of self-evaluation, though at times unsettling, has been necessary for my personal growth and the attainment of genuine fulfillment.

The word within 'ME' resonates on a deeply emotional level, offering profound insights into the human condition and our shared experiences. It transcends gender, age, and societal expectations, speaking directly to the core of our being.

It reminds us that the quest for inner peace and self-acceptance is universal, and that true fulfillment lies not in the pursuit of external validation but in unwavering acceptance and love for oneself.

Through its pages, "Facing Ernest Porter" guides us on a poignant journey of self-discovery, illuminating the path to finding solace within our own hearts. It prompts us to question our beliefs, challenge our assumptions, and confront the narratives that have shaped our identities.

It invites us to embrace vulnerability and embrace the discomfort that accompanies genuine self-reflection, for it is within those moments of unease that we uncover our most authentic selves.

In a society that often values external achievements over inner contentment, "Facing Ernest Porter" stands as a testament to the power of self-exploration and the pursuit of inner peace. Its pages are a refuge for those seeking a deeper understanding of themselves and a source of inspiration for anyone longing to embark on a journey of self-discovery.

So, to all the men, women, boys, and girls who yearn for a sense of fulfillment and seek to make peace with their true selves, "Facing Ernest Porter" is an essential read. It holds the potential to spark profound introspection, provoke meaningful conversations, and ultimately guide us toward a more authentic and gratifying existence.

It reminds us that our worth is not defined by external standards, but by the unapologetic embrace of our own unique and

Facing Ernest Porter

beautifully flawed selves." "Facing Ernest Porter" takes readers on a transformative odyssey, unraveling the layers of our being and unraveling the intricate tapestry of our lives. It ventures into unexplored territories of self-awareness, where comfort is stripped away, and the raw truth emerges.

The pages of "Facing Ernest Porter" offer a sanctuary for introspection, a safe space to confront the insecurities, doubts, and fears that often lurk in the shadows. It encourages us to delve into the depths of our emotions, giving voice to our joys, sorrows, hopes, and disappointments. Through this process, we gain a deeper understanding of ourselves, our values, and our true aspirations.

By shedding light on our vulnerabilities, "Facing Ernest Porter" enables us to embrace our imperfections and find solace within our own skin. It reminds us that true fulfillment comes not from conforming to societal expectations or seeking external validation, but from a profound acceptance of our authentic selves.

In a world that constantly bombards us with ideals of perfection, "Facing Ernest Porter" serves as an attestation that our worth lies in our uniqueness and individual journey.

Reading "Facing Ernest Porter" is an act of courage, as it challenges us to question the narratives we have constructed around our identities. It urges us to examine the influences that have shaped us, encouraging a critical appraisal of our beliefs, biases, and prejudices. By peering beyond the veil of comfort, we uncover hidden truths, liberating ourselves from the constraints of societal conditioning. Through its emotional prose, "Facing Ernest Porter" paints a vivid portrait of the human experience, one that resonates with readers of all ages and backgrounds.

It speaks to the shared struggles, triumphs, and desires that connect us on a fundamental level. It reminds us that we are not alone in our pursuit of inner peace and that our personal journeys intertwine with the collective tapestry of humanity.

This book serves as a compass, guiding us towards self-gratification that is rooted in genuine self-discovery. It teaches us to seek fulfillment not through external achievements or material possessions but by nurturing our inner selves, cultivating meaningful relationships, and aligning our actions with our core values.

In a world that often glorifies busyness and external achievements, "Facing Ernest Porter" invites us to slow down, reflect, and embark on a profound inward journey. It urges us to listen to the whispers of our souls, to honor our intuition, and to embrace the discomfort that accompanies growth and self-transformation.

So, whether you are a man, woman, boy, or girl, "Facing So, Ernest Porter" is an invaluable companion on the quest for self-understanding and inner peace. Its words have the power to ignite a spark within, illuminating the path toward authenticity, self-acceptance, and a life lived on one's own terms.

Ernest Porter

Introduction

In my quest to achieve life's greatest accomplishment, I found myself in an uncomfortable situation while standing in front of the mirrors of life. I had a challenging time defining the image that stared back at me.

The reflection I should have known the most about was the one I understood the least. To gain true knowledge and understanding, I realized I needed to embark on a journey of self-truth and accountability, even if it meant facing challenges along the way.

I came to the realization that the world is filled with countless selfishness, unjust conditions that causes people to lose themselves and value, but there is only one unique "you." While it is often said that God created us equal, nobody ever told me that we weren't equally created.

This realization implies that while we may all have equal inherent value and dignity as human beings, we each possess unique qualities, talents, and attributes that set us apart from one another.

To utterly understand ourselves and embrace our individuality, we must be willing to explore the depths of our being, face our fears, and acknowledge our shortcomings.

It is through self-reflection, self-awareness, and self-acceptance that we can grow and evolve into the best versions of ourselves.

Facing Ernest Porter

The journey towards self-discovery and understanding may not always be easy. It may involve confronting our own insecurities, weaknesses, and past mistakes.

However, by crossing the burning sands of self-truth and accountability, we can uncover our true essence and unlock our fullest potential.

Remember that you are a unique and valuable individual, with your own set of strengths, passions, and dreams. Embrace your individuality and use it as a guiding light to navigate through life's challenges. By doing so, you can achieve the greatest accomplishment of all: becoming the best version of yourself.

As I continued my journey of self-discovery, I delved deeper into the burning sands of self-truth and accountability. It was not an easy path to walk, as it required me to confront my deepest fears, insecurities, and doubts. The mirror of life reflected not only my physical appearance but also the layers of my being that I had kept hidden from myself.

I realized that understanding oneself is a lifelong process, a continuous exploration of our thoughts, emotions, and actions. It is a journey that demands honesty, vulnerability, and a willingness to challenge our preconceived notions. I had to let go of the masks I had worn to fit into societal expectations and confront the person I truly was underneath.

Ernest Porter

In this pursuit of self-truth, I discovered that I am an intricate tapestry woven from my experiences, beliefs, and relationships. I am the accumulation of my triumphs and failures, my joys and sorrows. Embracing my imperfections and acknowledging my mistakes became essential steps on this path toward self-understanding.

Through self-accountability, I accepted responsibility for my actions and their consequences. I recognized that my choices, both big and small, shape the person I become. Instead of blaming external circumstances or others, I took ownership of my life and the impact I have on those around me.

As I journeyed through the burning sands, I also learned the importance of self-compassion. I discovered that understanding oneself goes hand in hand with showing kindness and forgiveness to oneself. It is through this compassion that we can heal the wounds that hinder our growth and move forward with a renewed sense of purpose.

In the midst of my quest, I encountered moments of clarity and revelation. The image that stared back at me in the mirrors of life became clearer and more defined. I saw not only my flaws and vulnerabilities but also my strengths and potential. I began to embrace the uniqueness of my being, understanding that my individuality is a gift that adds richness to the world.

Facing Ernest Porter

In the end, I realized that while God may have created us equal in inherent worth, we are each uniquely fashioned with our own set of talents, passions, and purpose. It is through the understanding and acceptance of this truth that we can genuinely appreciate the diversity of humanity and the beauty of our individuality.

So, I encourage you to embark on your own journey of self-discovery, my friend. Stand before the mirrors of life with courage and curiosity. Embrace the discomfort, for it is in the discomfort that true growth occurs. Facing the discomfort of self-truth and accepting accountability for our actions take us to a place that allows us to develop a mentality to come to know and understand the extraordinary person that we are.

Chapter 1
The Awakening

What is an awakening? The awakening is a moment in time when someone's eyes are open to the reality that what they thought was righteous and true is false and has been manipulated for someone else's self-gain. In this realm of shadows, where echoes whisper and memories linger, a young soul named Ernest wandered aimlessly through the corridors of existence. His heart, burdened by the weight of unfulfilled dreams, yearned for a purpose greater than the empty facades that surrounded him.

One fateful morning, as the sun painted the sky with hues of gold and crimson, Ernest stood before a mirror that held the reflection of his weary soul. His eyes, once filled with vibrant hope, now reflected a world wearied by the masks he wore to fit in. The mirror became a portal, inviting him to confront the essence of his being, to unravel the truth that lay hidden beneath the layers of pretense.

Silent words escaped his lips, dancing in the air like ethereal whispers, as he pondered the profound question: "What can I tell this image in the mirror? Would it be the same lie I display to the world, and have it believe it?" The mirror, devoid of deceit, demanded authenticity, unmasking the facade and revealing the vulnerable truth within.

Ernest Porter

A symphony of emotions swelled within my chest, a chorus of doubts, fears, and insecurities that had haunted me for far too long.

The generational effects of oppressive mental brainwashing my family had endured had taken its toll, causing me to question my own worth and purpose. The relentless societal conditioning had fostered an identity crisis, forcing me to lose sight of the brilliance within my own essence.

But in this moment of self-confrontation, I found solace in the resounding words of my own conscious voice, a voice that refused to be silenced any longer. It spoke with tenderness and compassion, urging me to embrace my true self, to recognize the beauty that resided in the depths of his being.

"The journey to self-acceptance is not a sin or punishment," the voice gently whispered. "It is an act of liberation, an embrace of your own authenticity. You, dear Ernest, are worthy of love, compassion, and understanding just as any other living soul."

Tears welled in my eyes as I pondered the weight of these words. The simplicity of the "Facing Ernest" message resonated deep within my core. It shattered the illusion that I was destined to despise anything that resembled my own reflection, replacing it with a call to embrace my heritage, my culture, and my individuality.

With newfound determination, I accepted the responsibility

to embark on a quest to redefine my existence. I would no longer allow the world's projections to dictate my self-worth. Instead, I would stand before myself, resolute and unyielding, shaping my life based on God's instructions and my own terms.

Without a doubt, I knew that the path to personal growth demanded introspection and self-love. It required peeling back the layers of conditioning, dismantling the walls of self-doubt, and rewriting the narrative of my own life. With each step I took, I would transform pain into purpose, forging his own destiny from the raw materials of his unique experiences.

The journey would be arduous as he faced the demons of self-blame and the shackles of comparison. Yet, Ernest understood that his love for himself would be the beacon that guided him through the darkest nights, illuminating the path to self-discovery.

In the hallowed chambers of his soul, Ernest made a solemn vow to stand tall and unwavering. He would no longer be an impersonator, wearing masks to appease the expectations of others. Instead, he would embrace his authentic self, allowing his true essence to radiate like a beacon of light.

As I stepped away from the mirror, I carried within me the seeds of change. The world would bear witness to the transformation of a soul who dared to face himself, to break free from the bonds of inner oppression and external voices of distractions.

Just as the sun kissed the horizon, casting its golden hues across the landscape, a profound sense of awakening enveloped my heart. It was as if the universe whispered secrets to my soul, urging me to embark on a transformative journey.

In the depths of my being, I grappled with a haunting image that stared back at me from the mirror each day—a reflection that seemed distant, unfamiliar. The weight of societal expectations had pressed upon my spirit, leaving me feeling like an impersonator in my own life.

This is a feeling that more than I can attest to if a person is true to themselves. But today, everything would change. Today, I vowed to unravel the tapestry of my existence and discover the essence of my true self.

Despite my shortcomings, failures, and sense of hopelessness I once felt. No longer would the perception of others define me; instead, I would forge a path guided by self-assurance and the purpose God has created for me. If God could forgive a sinful world, who am I not to have enough compassion to forgive myself?

With each step, I began to shed the shackles of doubt and allowed his inner voice of value and purpose to soar. Like a melody weaving through the air, my thoughts danced around in my head with the rhythm of self-discovery.

Facing Ernest Porter

Embracing this unique identity became my liberation, and my once rebellion against a world that sought to confine me, was no more! Just like Romans 12:2 instructs us to "Be ye transformed by the renewing of your mind, that ye may prove what is that good, and acceptable, and perfect, will of God," I sought to change my way of thinking to change my direction in life.

In the quietude of this new mind, I posed a question to the reflection before me. Could a person live their entire life under the shadow of falsity and shame? How can we awaken a new image and love for ourselves after years of mental abuse? The mirror, a silent confidant, offered no pretense, compelling me to confront his deepest truths.

Do I owe people in my past apologies? Most definitely! Have I made enemies out of once friends? Probably, but do I bast in the sorrow and pity of those inconsistencies and bad choices? I pray not.

This man's journey in life is not without its battles, heartaches, pains, and disappointments. Oftentimes in our lives, inner demons whispered tales of unworthiness, their insidious tendrils threatening to undermine one's progress.

Yet, amidst the struggle, I realized the profound impact of my existence—a narrative often marginalized, diminished, or distorted by people closest to me.

Facing Ernest, the mirror of introspection, served as a canvas for me to paint my own story. It demanded an unwavering commitment to authenticity, and an unwavering acceptance of my heritage and experiences. It was a testament to the resilience of my spirit and the capacity to shape my own destiny.

In a world that sought to demoralize the Black community, I recognized the need to love myself even more, and my parents unconditionally, plus embrace my heritage as a Black man with a sense of pride on the same plane as other nationalities.

The journey toward self-appreciation demanded gratitude—gratitude for being God's creation, gratitude for the divine blueprint imprinted upon my soul, and an immeasurable respect for my mother.

Amidst my contemplation, I turned to the wisdom of generations past. I delved into the mercies of God, seeking a deeper understanding of my purpose. No longer content with superficial belief, I yearned for a connection that transcended imitation.

No matter how many obstacles people throw in my pathway, despite the back door conversation of negative discourse, I will press on!

Now, I began to understand that my mission in life was not to mimic the lives of others but to cultivate a legacy borne from my unique essence. Just as Darwin revealed the power of adaptability, I embraced the notion that my true strength lay in embracing

Facing Ernest Porter

change—a metamorphosis that shattered the illusions of conformity. Are we so easily submissive to being conformed or complying with another self-proclaimed authority? Should we not be on a journey to finding ourselves through the clear lens of truth and compliance with God? You may think that I'm speaking from a place of hope or dreams, but in the realm of dreams, I discovered the power to rewrite my narrative. Don Miguel Ruiz's words resonated deeply: the human mind was a constant dreamer. It dreamed of a future molded by individual choices, not by the expectations of others. And so, I embarked on a journey of self-reflection, turning the pages of my life. Examining the intricate details etched upon my soul. Today, I sought to redefine success to create a story that epitomized my uniqueness. No longer the scribe of others' accomplishments, I've aspired to be the author of my own destiny.

For those who observed this transformation, I posed a question: Would they recognize me beyond material possessions and societal roles? Would they appreciate the essence of my being, the authenticity I exuded? I knew that true fulfillment lay in living a life that resonated with my deepest truths.

With a determined heart and a resolute mind, I decided to embark on a path less traveled—a path of self-acceptance, empowerment, and love. Each step I took infused my existence with purpose and beauty, painting a masterpiece of resilience, determination, and unwavering authenticity.

Ernest Porter

As I began to let this new light shine, it led me to venture further into the unknown. My spirit ablaze with the fire of transformation, I vowed to leave a legacy—a testament to the power of change, the courage to break free from societal expectations, and the beauty that emerges when one embraces their true self.

The ringing tones of a man whose name resonated with the echoes of forgotten legends, stood before the mirror, his reflection a haunting reminder of his own journey.

In the depths of my soul, I battled against inner demons that whispered doubts and insecurities into my every thought because no matter how great your intentions are or how valuable your message may be, so often when people write from a Black perspective, the respect is not like other people who tell their lives on paper. They feel like they've got to add a special sauce, so it has a juicy flavor."

But this is no ordinary message! It delved into the complexities of identity, exploring the trauma that had been woven into the fabric of my existence. Our minds have been conditioned to harbor ill will against each other, then the unexplainable self-hatred that's extending to anything that resembled me. It was a toxic cycle, perpetuated by societal expectations and my own internal struggles.

In the depths of my self-discovery, I questioned my worthiness. Was I merely a product of my parents' shortcomings? Did I have the strength to rise above the circumstances that had shaped me? These questions gnawed at my spirit, threatening to consume me.

Facing Ernest was a journey that demanded courage and self-reflection. It beckoned me to stand before the mirror and engage in a heartfelt conversation with my own reflection, which, by now, I began not to recognize. It was in these quiet moments that I sought to draw a realistic image of the person I aspired to become, using relatable examples of resilience and growth. I had to break free from the shackles of comparison. The world is filled with deceptive mirages, tempting people to doubt their own innate worth. But I knew that God's love for me must be nurtured, born from a deep appreciation for the unique creation that I was.

Only God held the blueprint of my identity, and it was time for me to embrace it fully. One of the most feared obstacles in a man's life is that image that looks back at him every morning and every night. How can I spend my entire life as an impersonator of someone who doesn't spend one thought thinking about what's best for me?

This is not just something to write about but a reality that millions of people face each day! I asked myself this question: If you really want to get to a certain place in life, what are you doing to change your life and your circumstances? The first thing that came to mind is that there should never be a person who values you more than you!

I'm not talking about being egotistical, but this is about assurance of who I'm created to be. Once I could catch a glimpse of why I was created and what my passion was, then I began walking in my footprint of life and not others. As I leaped into a new way of seeing myself, it pushed me on this introspective journey, and I was reminded of Jesus' mission to restore a broken covenant. It served as a poignant reminder that he, too, had a purpose to fulfill.

Even though Jesus asked, "Let this cup pass from me," He knew that there was a purpose greater than himself, and his focus was far greater than a human man, and his dedication to unlocking God's plan for redemption is the least respected gift to the world.

Something Charles Darwin said registered in my mind: "he was not the strongest or most intelligent person who survived, but rather the most adaptable to change." This realization made me take a step back and reshaped my thinking.

Here stood all 6ft 2" 220 pounds of myself with a new methodology that I understood and that I needed to embrace change, to let go of the societal masks I had worn for so long.

Don Miguel Ruiz's wisdom added another layer of understanding. The human mind was always dreaming, whether awake or asleep. It was in these dreams that I needed to find clarity about my past, present, and future.

What was I truly dreaming about? What was my vision? Was I

driven by a desire to become the best version of myself, or was I consumed by envy and greed to get what others had? Facing Ernest is a journey devoted to peeling back the layers of my life, exploring the fine print that proclaimed equality and individual specialty. I hope that others can be inspired to challenge themselves in the face of truth.

How would one respond to their own self-induced oppression? I want to open the world's eyes to the destruction we bring upon ourselves for not being who we are. I now began to ponder the authenticity of the relationships around me.

Did they appreciate me for who I truly was, or were they enamored with the roles I played in their lives? How many people called me to see how I'm doing, or does it take for me to make the first call? A pivotal moment had arrived. I had to stop and think because I needed to ask myself if I was closer to finding myself and if I was closer to success or failure. It was time for a reset, a reboot of my trajectory.

Like a computer in need of an escape from a stagnant condition, I had to hit my own reset button. This would allow me to redefine what story I was writing with my life. How would I be remembered? It was time to leave a legacy that celebrated my uniqueness.

In the beginning, this journey might not be pretty. It might unveil truths I was reluctant to face. But I understood that sometimes, one had to take a shower even if they didn't feel dirty. Self-doubt, Guilt, and emptiness would no longer hold me captive. With each step forward, my heart surged with a newfound sense of purpose. The scars that marked my past were now reminders of resilience, badges of honor that bore witness to the battles I had fought and the victories I had won. No longer a victim, I emerged as the hero of my own story. The reflection in the mirror began to shift. It was no longer a mere image; it was a testament to the transformative power of self-acceptance and love. This man's eyes radiated with a renewed sense of hope, my spirit soaring on the wings of possibility.

Not afraid to stumble, not sensitive to criticism or the jealousy of others who want to reclaim themselves but succumb to peer pressure and an extinguished flame of potential.

And so, the journey continued, fueled by the realization that change was not only possible but necessary! With each passing day, I'm etching my truth onto the pages of my life's story, a narrative that celebrates growth, authenticity, and the audacity to face oneself. With each waking moment, I'm more motivated to create a remarkable day. Now, I smiled at the reflection staring back at me. My soul has awakened from the slumber of self-doubt and has stepped onto a path that promised a life lived in full, vibrant color, where every step was a testament to the beauty of embracing change. In the depths of my soul, I relentlessly whispered my mantra, the essence of my journey encapsulated in three simple words: "I am enough." And with those words, I write on blank pages that become a new chapter, ready to weave my story with threads of resilience, purpose, and self-love.

What it balls down to is that I woke up to the corners of my mind and accepted that with sacrifices comes misunderstanding and hurt from those I love. I don't want to wake up one day and look in the mirror and not recognize who's looking back at me!

An elderly man asked me, how often do you speak blessings over your days and nights, speak power over your life, and tell yourself you are greater than what somebody says or over your family? I tossed in my bed for days as these questions seemed easy and simple, but they were much more than that. Meaning, how could I speak with assurance when I was not comfortable in my direction?

That was one of those pivotal moments in life my grandmother talked about. It sparked a movement in my life that started me walking alone down the steep stairs of my inner consciousness and coming face-to-face with my greatest adversary.

Here is a question that I propose to you today: What can you tell this image in the mirror, the same lie I display to the world, and he believes it? When that image can't lie or impersonate that of something else, it must reveal that which is what it is. Just imagine if the voice of your consciousness could speak back to you every time you stand before a mirror. What would it say?

The mental brainwashing and infection that spread through the minds of our young children are found hard to cure and reprogram. This conditioning made me feel compelled to just accepting things as it was and who I am was a sin and punishment. I was a young man fighting inner demons for my very existence in a world of destruction, manipulation, and lies.

This is another ingredient of the fuel identity crisis, and It's so easy to demoralize people in their traumatic state and affect every aspect of their lives moving forward.

The simplicity of Facing Ernest's message is 'Yes, Black people suffer trauma, love their families and culture just like any other living soul ... but we have been conditioned to harbor so much ill will that we hate anything that looks like us, to the degree that we will destroy that image with no remorse. I remember the looks I got from people in various towns and cities in this country, and it convinced me that the entire world was against me, and nobody could protect me or my family from this pain.

So, I continuously had to keep working on myself, not to fit into that world of confusion but into a space where I'm making a real-life decision on who I want to be! I didn't want to know my character only because a character can be described as a person who says or does funny or unusual things. I wanted to search out God's building blocks for humanity and how do I continually turn my pain into purpose?

Facing Ernest Porter

Like my grandmother would say," Making something out of nothing." I began to develop this energy to drive my feet to the edge of the bed and firmly plant them on the floor each day!

I questioned myself repeatedly, Like, what are you going to do once you stand up? What commitment or agreement will I make with myself that will formulate and move people out of my life so positive people can enter my life?

We must investigate the deepest part of our soul and provide an intellectual justification of our worthiness, not based on someone else painted picture or your unsatisfactory feeling about yourself but solely on an appreciation for the special creation of God Almighty!

What happens when you secretly hate and blame your parents for your shortcomings or lack of drive and vision, which leaves you with an arguing spirit because nothing else has worked.

These emotions or phases of so-called helplessness can be crushing, especially if you have given up on yourself.

"Facing Ernest Porter" brings you face to face with you so that you can stand in the mirror and make a non-influential argument with yourself in that quiet time and draw a realistic image of whatever you want to become from accessible and relatable examples of what productive building blocks to successful life looks like.

But the question in Facing Ernest is, what story are you writing? How will people remember you? Are you the scribe for other's actions and accomplishments or leaving a legacy that describes your uniqueness? There should come a time in your life when you ask yourself this: What am I closest to, success or failure?

And then hit reboot so you can reset your trajectory! Just like a computer has the keys control/Alt/Delete when your system is stuck and may need a hard reboot! This restart is the requirement to get you out of the condition you're in. When is the last time you hit your reset button? Have you ever asked someone, "What were you thinking"? But have you ever asked yourself, "What am I doing?"

The mission of Facing Ernest is dedicated to facing the reality of my own trials, making my life whole, and elevating those around me in a way that encourages others to live in their truth. How to prepare for your future, and how to mentally prepare for that discovery because it isn't always pretty in the beginning. Some people don't take a shower when they don't think they are dirty, and don't feel guilty or empty when they don't think anything is wrong.

Chapter 2
Embracing Your Worth

This chapter began with a powerful reminder that there should never be a person who values me more than I do! It emphasized the importance of self-assurance and recognizing the unique purpose for which everyone's created.

As I absorbed these words, I understood that I needed to walk in my own footsteps rather than following the paths of others.

I started by embracing who I am inwardly as well as what the world sees, outspoken and encouraged. I did something my grandmother used to do for me: speak blessings over myself day and night.

Speaking power into my very existence, breathing life into my inner soul, was something new. Then morphed a belief in myself that stamped my own worthiness. I felt the power to reject the limiting conditions imposed upon me by society and, roll up my sleeves of wisdom and knowledge, and to embrace my true potential.

As I delved deeper into the pages of my spirit, emotions stirred within me like a tempestuous storm. The words resonated in the depths of my soul, igniting a fire that had long been dormant. The journey of self-discovery had begun, and I could no longer ignore the call to embrace my worth as a man.

Around every street corner and hallway of life, I confronted the demons of my past that had plagued my mind, whispering tales of inadequacy and self-doubt.

The mental brainwashing that had infected my thoughts was exposed, its power dwindling in the face of truth. No longer would I succumb to the illusion that accepting the color of my skin was a sin or a punishment.

These thoughts and emotional conversations with myself penetrated my mind day after day, revealing the profound impact of demoralization and trauma on the lives of Black individuals.

The weight of societal conditioning pressed heavily upon my shoulders, but I refused to be crushed. With each step through life conformed into sentence upon sentence, I shed the chains that held my mind captive, reclaiming my identity with unyielding strength.

In the crucible of self-reflection, I confronted the ghosts of my past, the blame and resentment I had harbored for my father. Once I realized that I alone held the power to shape my destiny, to transform my ignorance and pain into purpose.

The journey ahead was daunting, but I took solace in the wisdom of my grandmother, who taught me to take very things that others find no value and make them something of value, even its only to me. The revelations of writing this book encouraged me to look beyond the superficial measures of success, to question the role I played in impersonating others rather than embracing my unique essence.

The long brushed-off words of my mother began to make sense in my mind, reminding me that adaptability and self-acceptance were the keys to survival and growth.

When do I plant both feet firmly on the ground, root my life based on the things most valuable to me, and shy away from the dreaming mind that makes others lose their sense of reality? I contemplated the dreams I had been nurturing, the visions of a future where I could truly be myself.

No longer would I be confined by the expectations of others, locked in a confined space, or the illusions of comparative study! My dreams would become my reality, and my reality would reflect the authenticity of my soul. With each passing chapter, my spirit soared higher, fueled by the flickering flame of self-love and gratitude. Now, I'm growing mentally and understand that my love for myself has never been based on external comparisons but only on an appreciation for the divine masterpiece I was.

The blueprint of my identity lay in the hands of a higher power, and I surrendered to its guidance. I asked myself, for what was I designed? I knew there was a special mission that lay before me, no matter how hard I tried to run away from it. How could I use my voice to have a valuable impact on the lives of others once I fully embraced my true self?

Ernest Porter

It challenged me to break free from the confines of imitation and create a legacy that celebrated an undeniable uniqueness. The pen became my instrument and my life, the canvas on which I would change the lives of others through honest compassion and my own story.

With determination burning in his eyes, Ernest vowed to pour out words etched deep within his heart. He vowed to honor his journey of self-discovery, to navigate the rough waters of transformation with unwavering courage. No longer would he be content with a life of mediocrity; he would rise above, leaving a legacy that defied all expectations.

Embracing his worth, Ernest took his first step into the unknown, his path illuminated by the flickering light of self-assurance. The journey would be challenging, but he knew deep within that the power to change his life lay within his own hands.

And so, with a resolute spirit and a heart brimming with hope, he ventured forth into a world where his true self would shine, unapologetically and authentically.

The weight of self-doubt had been cast aside, replaced by the armor of self-belief, as he dared to dream and dared to be. In the quiet moments of solitude, he had discovered his own strength, and in the cheers of his closest allies, he found the wind beneath his wings.

Facing Ernest Porter

Ernest's journey was not merely a passage through time and space but a pilgrimage into the core of his being. Each step he took was a declaration, a testament to the resilience of the human spirit and the boundless potential within. The world might challenge him, but it could not deter him, for he had discovered the fire within that no storm could extinguish.

In this new chapter of his life, he wasn't just writing his own story; he was living it! With every word spoken and every action taken, he painted his narrative with the vivid colors of authenticity. With every hurdle, he would rise, and with every setback, he would learn! The canvas of his life awaited, ready to be adorned with the masterpiece of his true self.

Ernest's journey was a symphony of courage, a testament to the enduring human spirit, and an anthem of hope for those who might follow in his footsteps. As he moved forward into the uncharted, he knew that he was not alone; he carried the dreams and aspirations of everyone who had ever dared to embrace their worth and shine their unique light.

In the tapestry of life, Ernest's story wove a beautiful thread, a testament to the magic that could unfold when one embraced their own worth. With every sunrise, he saw the world with fresh eyes, painted in the hues of his newfound self-assurance. The challenges were not obstacles; they were opportunities to prove to himself and the world that he was capable of greatness.

His heart, once a timid whisper, had now transformed into a powerful song, singing the melodies of his soul. Ernest understood that the world was vast, and the path ahead held both valleys of darkness and peaks of light. But he walked it, not in fear, but with a burning determination that illuminated his way.

With each step, he redefined what was possible, not just for himself but for all those who saw in his journey a reflection of their own unspoken desires. He became a source of inspiration, a living embodiment of the potential that resided within each of us.

The world welcomed Ernest's authentic self, for it recognized the rare beauty of someone unafraid to be truly themselves. In the vulnerability of his authenticity, he found strength, and in the love of those who appreciated him, he found affirmation.

As he continued forward, he knew that the road would still have its share of trials, but he had the tools and the tenacity to overcome them. His heart, brimming with hope, was a beacon to others who might be taking their first steps into the unknown, a testament that it was not just okay to be oneself but a cause for celebration.

Facing Ernest Porter

Ernest's journey was a love letter to self-discovery, a hymn to resilience, and an emotional masterpiece of unwavering belief. He wrote his story not just with words but with every action, every moment of courage, and every smile that reflected the joy of embracing his worth. In doing so, he ignited a flame of inspiration that would burn bright for generations to come.

Ernest's journey was a symphony of emotions, an ode to the power of self-discovery and the resilience of the human spirit. The pages of his life were filled with moments of laughter and tears, of triumph and defeat. He learned that the essence of life was not just in reaching the destination but in savoring every step of the journey.

As he moved forward, he held on to the lessons he had learned along the way. He cherished the warmth of friendship, the embrace of love, and the courage to face his inner demons. In the mirror of self-reflection, he saw not just his own reflection but the countless faces of those who had walked beside him, lending their strength to his cause.

Ernest's story was a reminder that we are all explorers on this unpredictable voyage called life. It was a testament that we have the power to change, to evolve, and to uncover the diamonds buried within our own souls.

With every sunrise, he was reborn, ready to face the world anew. The uncertainties ahead didn't fill him with fear but with a sense of adventure. For in embracing his worth and living authentically, he had found the magic that transforms ordinary existence into an extraordinary journey.

The world watched in awe as Ernest continued to write his story, one word at a time, one experience at a time. His narrative inspired others to look within, to embark on their own adventures of self-discovery, and to embrace their worth with open hearts.

Ernest's journey was more than a personal quest; it was a message to humanity. It said, "You are more than your doubts. You are more than your fears. You are a universe of potential waiting to be explored, and the world is waiting to embrace the real you."

In every chapter of his life, in every challenge, and in every triumph, Ernest's story echoed the profound truth that embracing our worth and living authentically is a journey worth taking, for it leads not just to self-fulfillment but to a brighter, more compassionate, and more genuine world for us all.

Chapter 3
Grateful Reflection Journey

We spend so much energy running from the very person we can't hide from, ourselves. Now, I had to pen down the most thought-provoking question: What if the voice of your consciousness could speak back to you every time you stood in front of a mirror? Imagine pondering this idea and envision the raw honesty and self-reflection that would emerge.

As I stood toe-to-toe with myself and engaged in these conversations with my own reflection. To truly see myself for who I was, beyond the lies and masks, and to embrace my authentic self.

Through these dialogues, I would uncover the inner demons that plagued me as a child and unknowingly as an adult, but God has a way of teaching us unteachable things that inspired me to push ahead and learn to reconcile with his past.

With a determined heart and strong hands, Ernest picked up the pen of his soul, ready to etch his dreams upon the blank pages of his existence. The ink of his emotions flowed freely, staining the parchment with the hues of his passion and purpose.

No longer would he allow others to dictate his story; he would wield the power of his own voice, crafting a tale that resonated with his very being.

Ernest Porter

In the quiet solitude of his room, Ernest immersed himself in the process of self-discovery. He peeled back the layers of societal expectations, shedding the weight of others' opinions that had burdened his spirit for far too long.

This life we experience is not the property of others to dictate or oppress but for us to enjoy in our own way, in our own journey. Why must I be reminded that my life was an empty canvas, awaiting the strokes of my true earthly experience?

With each stroke of the pen, Ernest unraveled the essence of his being. He delved into the depths of his soul, unearthing forgotten dreams and hidden talents.

He discovered that his story was not restricted by the boundaries of his past or the doubts that had once imprisoned him. It was a story of resilience, of triumph over adversity, and of the infinite possibilities that lay before him.

The words flowed like a river, carrying with them the essence of his hopes, fears, and aspirations. He wrote of love, not just the romantic kind, but love for himself, his family, and humanity.

He penned tales of compassion, empathy, and the desire to have influence in the lives of others. His story became a tapestry woven with threads of authenticity and vulnerability.

Facing Ernest Porter

As the ink spilled onto the page, Ernest's emotions swirled in a symphony of joy and sorrow. He confronted his deepest wounds, acknowledging the pain that had shaped him and transformed it into fuel for his growth. Each word became a cathartic release, healing the scars that had lingered silently within his heart.

Through the act of writing, Ernest discovered the power of his voice. I heard the screams that raced through the chambers of his soul, resonating with a newfound strength and conviction.

He realized that his story was not just his own; it had the potential to touch the lives of others, to inspire and ignite the flames of their own self-discovery.

In the dim glow of the night, Ernest's pen danced across the pages, breathing life into the characters of his narrative. He wrote of resilience, of overcoming adversity, and of finding beauty during chaos.

His story embraced the depths of human experience, embracing both the shadows and the light that defined his journey.

As the final words found their place on the parchment, Adam's heart swelled with a profound sense of accomplishment.

He had become the protagonist of his own story, the architect of his destiny. With each chapter, he would continue to evolve, grow, and redefine the narrative of his existence.

The book had served as a guiding compass, illuminating the path that lay before him. It had taught him that writing his story was not a linear process but a perpetual dance between introspection and action. As Adam closed the book, he understood that the real adventure had just begun—a life filled with purpose, authenticity, and the unwavering belief in the power of his own story.

Ernest's contemplation of the voice of his consciousness speaking back to him in front of a mirror raises intriguing possibilities. Imagine the raw honesty and self-reflection that would emerge if our inner thoughts and reflections could be vocalized.

It would provide a unique opportunity to truly see ourselves beyond the facades and masks we wear, enabling us to embrace our authentic selves.

In these imagined dialogues with his own reflection, Ernest sought to uncover the inner demons that haunted him, both in his childhood and unknowingly as an adult.

He acknowledged that confronting and reconciling with his past was a necessary step towards self-discovery and growth. Ernest recognized that despite the challenges and pains he had experienced, there was a greater purpose in his life from which he could learn.

With trepidation, Ernest embraced the pen, symbolizing his readiness to etch his dreams onto the blank pages of his existence. The ink, representing his emotions, flowed freely as he passionately expressed his desires and aspirations.

Facing Ernest Porter

No longer would he allow others to dictate his story; instead, he would assert the power of his own voice, crafting a narrative that resonated deeply with his being.

In the solace of his room, Ernest embarked on a journey of self-discovery. He shed the weight of societal expectations and opinions that had burdened his spirit for far too long, recognizing that his life was an empty canvas waiting for his truth to be expressed.

As he wrote, he unraveled the essence of his being, unearthing forgotten dreams and hidden talents. Ernest realized that his story wasn't restricted by the limitations of his past or the doubts that had once held him captive. It was a story of resilience, triumph, and limitless possibilities.

In the tranquil embrace of the night, Ernest's pen danced across the pages, breathing life into the characters of his narrative.

Chapter 4
Unravelling Self-Hatred

Your journey has brought you face to face with the powerful influence of mental brainwashing and societal conditioning. It takes great strength and courage to confront these ingrained beliefs and unravel their hold on your mind.

As a young man, the struggles you faced were unique and challenging as you sought to find help and understanding amidst a community where everyone was grappling with their own mental burdens.

In this quest for self-discovery, I gradually became aware of the deep-seated self-hatred that had been unconsciously instilled in me. This self-hatred extended beyond just my own identity; it permeated my perception of anything that resembled who I truly was.

This realization was undoubtedly painful, as it forced me to confront the ways in which I had been oppressed and disconnected from my authentic self.

However, this revelation also became a powerful catalyst for change. It ignited a fire within me to break free from the chains of oppression and reclaim my true essence. The recognition of my own conditioning opened the door to a journey of self-love and self-acceptance.

Facing Ernest Porter

Once I began to understand that healing and growth could only happen by shedding the layers of societal expectations and embracing my unique identity.

While it may feel like searching for a needle in a haystack to find guidance and support in a community where everyone is grappling with their own mental burdens, it's important to remember that you are not alone.

There are resources available, such as therapy, support groups, and online communities, where you can connect with others who are also on a journey of self-discovery and healing.

Remember to be patient and kind to yourself as you navigate this process. Breaking free from ingrained beliefs and conditioning takes time and effort, but with dedication and self-compassion, you can reclaim your authentic self and find a sense of belonging within your own community.

As you continue your journey of self-discovery and liberation, it's crucial to prioritize self-care and self-compassion. Healing from the weight of trauma and societal conditioning is a process that requires patience and understanding. Be gentle with yourself as you navigate the challenges and setbacks that may arise along the way.

One powerful tool in unraveling the chains of oppression and fostering self-love is education. Seek out knowledge and resources that challenge oppressive narratives and help you understand the roots of societal conditioning.

Expand your understanding of different perspectives, cultures, and identities. This broader awareness will not only empower you but also allow you to engage in meaningful conversations with others in your community who may be on similar journeys.

Surround yourself with supportive individuals who uplift and validate your experiences. Seek out communities, whether in-person or online, that prioritize healing and growth.

Connecting with others who have faced similar struggles can provide a sense of validation, understanding, and belonging.

Embrace practices that nurture your mental, emotional, and physical well-being. Explore mindfulness techniques, such as meditation or journaling, which allow you to connect with your inner self and cultivate self-awareness.

Engage in activities that bring you joy, whether it's creative expression, spending time in nature, or pursuing hobbies that ignite your passion.

Remember that healing is not a linear process. There may be moments when you feel overwhelmed or face setbacks, but these are opportunities for growth and resilience.

Facing Ernest Porter

Celebrate your progress, no matter how small, and honor the courage it takes to confront and dismantle the conditioning that once held you captive.

By shedding the layers of self-hatred and embracing self-love, you pave the way for a brighter future not just for yourself but also for those around you.

As you reclaim your true essence, you become an inspiration and a beacon of hope for others who may be trapped in the same patterns of oppression.

You are on a transformative path of self-discovery and empowerment. Embrace the journey and know that you have the strength within you to overcome the obstacles and embrace the beautiful, authentic individual that you are.

In your journey to confront mental brainwashing and societal conditioning, it's imperative to recognize that you have the power to rewrite your own narrative.

Challenge the negative self-talk and beliefs that have been ingrained in you. Replace them with positive affirmations and empowering thoughts. Remind yourself daily of your worth and embrace the uniqueness of your identity.

As you work towards breaking free from the chains of oppression, consider seeking professional help. A therapist or counselor can provide guidance, support, and tools to navigate the complexities of trauma and self-discovery.

They can help you process your emotions, develop coping strategies, and foster self-compassion. Remember that reaching out for assistance is a sign of strength, not weakness.

Engage in activities that promote self-care and nurture your well-being. This can include engaging in regular exercise, practicing mindfulness and relaxation techniques, nourishing your body with healthy food, and ensuring you get enough rest and sleep. Prioritize activities that bring you joy and allow you to express yourself authentically.

Journaling can be a powerful tool for self-reflection and self-expression. Write down your thoughts, emotions, and reflections on your journey.

Use this space to explore your identity, process your experiences, and document your growth. You may be surprised at the insights and clarity that can emerge from this practice.

As you shed the weight of societal conditioning, remember that you are not alone in this process. Seek out like-minded individuals who are also on a journey of self-discovery.

Connect with supportive communities, whether online or in-person, where you can share your experiences, learn from others, and find a sense of belonging. Building a network of understanding and compassionate individuals can provide invaluable support along your path.

Lastly, be patient with yourself. Healing and personal growth take time. Embrace the journey as a continuous process of self-discovery and transformation. Celebrate each milestone and acknowledge the progress you make, no matter how small it may seem.

You are embarking on a brave and empowering journey of reclaiming your true essence and cultivating self-love. Embrace the challenges and triumphs that lie ahead, and remember that you have the resilience and strength within you to overcome any obstacle. Believe in your own power to create a future filled with authenticity, self-acceptance, and love.

As you continue your path of self-discovery and liberation, remember to be kind and compassionate to yourself. Recognize that undoing years of conditioning and healing from trauma takes time and effort. It's okay to have setbacks and moments of doubt. Embrace them as opportunities for growth and learning.

During this journey, it can be helpful to develop a daily self-care routine. Dedicate time each day to activities that nourish your mind, body, and soul.

This could include meditation, practicing gratitude, engaging in creative pursuits, or spending time in nature. Prioritize self-care as a way to recharge and replenish your energy.

Seek out resources and literature that inspire and empower you. Educate yourself about the experiences of others who have overcome similar struggles and challenges.

This can provide validation, guidance, and a sense of connection. Remember, knowledge is a powerful tool in dismantling the oppressive narratives that have influenced your mindset.

Surround yourself with a supportive community of individuals who uplift and validate your journey. Seek out spaces where you can engage in meaningful conversations, share your experiences, and learn from others.

Cultivate relationships based on trust, empathy, and understanding. Together, you can create a safe and empowering environment where healing and growth flourish.

"Embrace your identity and practice self-love and self-acceptance as you unveil your true essence." Celebrate your strengths, talents, and uniqueness. Embrace the qualities that make you who you are.

Treat yourself with kindness, forgiveness, and understanding. Remember that you deserve love and respect, both from others and from yourself.

In your interactions with others, strive to promote compassion and empathy. Share your journey with those who are willing to listen and understand.

Facing Ernest Porter

Your authenticity and courage can inspire others to embark on their own paths of self-discovery and healing. By creating a ripple effect of positive change, you contribute to a community where collective growth and support can thrive.

Remember, this is your journey, and you have the power to shape it. Trust your intuition and follow the path that feels true to you. Embrace the challenges as opportunities for growth and transformation.

Believe in your inner strength and resilience, for they will guide you towards a life filled with authenticity, joy, and fulfillment.

You are on a remarkable journey of self-liberation and self-love. Embrace every step, celebrate your progress, and never forget the incredible power that lies within you.

As you delve deeper into your journey of self-liberation and self-love, it's essential to remember that you are not defined by the past or the conditioning that once held you captive. Embrace the present moment and focus on creating the future you desire.

Take time to reflect on your values, passions, and dreams. Connect with your innermost desires and aspirations. What brings you joy? What ignites your spirit? Align your actions and choices with the essence of who you truly are, allowing your authentic self to shine brightly.

Embrace the power of forgiveness, both for yourself and others. Release the burdens of resentment and grudges, allowing space for healing and growth. Forgiveness doesn't mean condoning harmful actions but rather freeing yourself from the negative energy that keeps you stuck in the past.

Practice gratitude to cultivate a positive mindset. Focus on the blessings, big and small, that surround you. Express appreciation for the progress you've made, the support you've received, and the opportunities that lie ahead. Gratitude opens the door to abundance and attracts more positivity into your life.

As you continue your journey, be open to learning and expanding your perspectives. Challenge your own beliefs and biases. Seek out diverse voices and experiences that broaden your understanding of the world. Engage in meaningful conversations that foster empathy, understanding, and unity.

Remember to be patient with yourself. Understanding that healing of past pain and growth are not linear processes but sequential steps in a task or process of embracing your jubilations and the tribulations, and life's moments of clarity and the moments of confusion.

Allow yourself to evolve and unfold naturally, trusting that you are on the right path towards self-discovery and self-fulfillment.

Celebrate the small victories along the way. Acknowledge

your progress, no matter how seemingly insignificant. Each step forward, no matter how small, brings you closer to living a life that is authentic and true to your heart.

Finally, as you reclaim your true essence, consider how you can contribute to creating a more compassionate and inclusive world. Advocate for the rights and well-being of others who have faced similar struggles.

Share your story, your insights, and your wisdom to inspire and uplift those around you. Your journey has the power to have influence, not only in your own life but in the lives of others as well.

Embrace this extraordinary journey of self-liberation and self-love. Trust yourself, follow your intuition, and know that you have the power to create a future filled with authenticity, joy, and fulfillment. Believe in the strength within you and continue to shine your light unapologetically.

Chapter 5
Reflections of Change

In the depths of "Reflections of Change," Ernest unearthed a profound chapter that resonated with the echoes of my soul—the chapter of transforming pain into purpose.

As he plunged into its pages, a surge of emotion welled within him, for he knew that within these words lay a beacon of hope, a guiding light to navigate the shadows of my past.

Ernest's inner voice intertwined with his grandmother's wisdom, painting a vivid tapestry of resilience and redemption.

His heart swelled with gratitude for the lessons imparted by his grandmother, a wise guardian who had weathered her own storms and emerged stronger on the other side.

His grandmother's words would always provide a sense of comfort in his mind, like a soothing melody in a world of chaos. She had taught him that true strength lay not in the absence of pain but in the ability to weave purpose from its threads.

In her gentle voice, she had shared the secret alchemy of making something out of nothing—a testament to the indomitable spirit that resided within each and every one of us.

Ernest's gaze fell upon the trials and tribulations that had woven their way through his life, leaving scars upon his heart.

Facing Ernest Porter

The wounds of his past whispered stories of anguish and disappointment, threatening to overshadow his dreams. But in the sanctuary of these written words, he found solace and inspiration.

The pages unfolded before him, revealing tales of ordinary people who had transformed their pain into purpose. They had stared adversity in the face and refused to be defined by it. Instead, they had harnessed their pain as a catalyst for change, as fuel to ignite the flames of their inner passion.

With each turn of the page, Ernest's own experiences flickered before his eyes—moments of heartache, shattered dreams, and the weight of unspoken burdens. But amidst the darkness, a flicker of hope emerged, a spark of recognition that his pain held the seeds of his purpose.

He realized that the key to his transformation lay not in blaming external circumstances or others for his wounds but in embracing his own power—the power to rise above, the power to rewrite his narrative. It was a profound realization that his drive and vision were not at the mercy of his past but were firmly rooted within the depths of his being.

Ernest felt a fire kindling within him—a fire of determination, of resilience, of unwavering faith in his own ability to shape his destiny. He understood that pain was not a punishment but a teacher—an invitation to dig deep, to excavate the treasures buried within his soul.

As he absorbed the wisdom of those who had walked this transformative path before him, Adam's perspective shifted. He began to see his pain as a wellspring of strength, a catalyst for growth. With every step forward, he embraced the beauty of the scars etched upon his heart, knowing that they were not symbols of weakness but badges of courage.

In this sacred chapter of "Reflections of Change," Ernest pledged to himself—to honor his pain by forging a purpose that would leave an indelible mark upon the world.

He would channel his experiences into empathy, his wounds into wisdom, and his struggles into building blocks toward a brighter tomorrow.

With renewed resolve, Ernest closed the chapter, carrying within him the torch of transformation. He knew that the journey ahead would not be without its challenges, but he also knew that he possessed the power to transcend them.

Armed with the wisdom of his grandmother and the stories of those who had walked this path, he stepped forward, embracing the alchemical dance of pain and purpose.

And as he embarked on this sacred pilgrimage, Ernest whispered a silent prayer of gratitude—for the pain that had sculpted him, for the purpose that awaited him, and for the boundless resilience that would carry him through.

Facing Ernest Porter

As Ernest delved deeper into the pages of "Reflections of Change," he stumbled upon a chapter that spoke directly to the depths of his soul—the chapter of transforming pain into purpose.

The words on the page danced before his eyes, resonating with a familiar ache within his heart. It was a poignant reminder that within the crucible of suffering lay the seeds of transformation and the power to create something extraordinary.

In the midst of his journey, Ernest recalled the wise words of his beloved grandmother, whose spirit had been a guiding light in his life. She had whispered to him in tender moments, her voice filled with the warmth of love and wisdom.

"Darling," she had said, "never underestimate the strength within you to turn pain into purpose. From the ashes of your struggles, you have the power to weave a tapestry of resilience and hope."

Those words echoed in Ernest's mind as he embarked on this transformative chapter. With each turn of the page, he glimpsed a path illuminated by possibility—a path that was not hindered by external circumstances or shackled by blame. It was a path woven by his own determination, his unwavering belief that he could rise above the ashes of adversity and create something meaningful.

The author's words gently embraced Ernest's weary heart, reminding him that pain was not an endpoint but a catalyst for growth. It was an invitation to dig deep into the caverns of his soul, where wounds lay hidden, waiting to transform into wellsprings of purpose.

With hesitant but hopeful steps, he allowed himself to confront the pain that had shaped his past, the scars that had etched their mark upon his being.

As Ernest began to peel back the layers of his experiences, he encountered the rawness of vulnerability. He traced the jagged contours of his pain, acknowledging the wounds that had left him broken and scarred.

Yet, within the depths of that pain, he discovered a wellspring of empathy—a profound understanding of the human condition, born from his own trials and tribulations.

In the crucible of his suffering, Ernest discovered that he possessed the power to transmute his pain into purpose. He realized that his story held the potential to touch the lives of others, to kindle a flicker of hope in hearts burdened by similar struggles.

With every page turned, he understood that his experiences were not in vain—they were the raw materials from which he would forge his purpose.

With newfound clarity, Ernest began to craft a narrative that defied the limitations of his pain. He embraced his struggles as a teacher, his wounds as reminders of his resilience.

No longer bound by the shackles of victimhood, he reimagined his story as a beacon of inspiration—a testament to the indomitable spirit that resides within the souls of each and every one of us.

Facing Ernest Porter

The author's voice whispered through the words on the page, urging Adam to wield his pain as a transformative tool. It was an invitation to let go of bitterness and resentment, to release the weight of past grievances.

With a heart brimming with forgiveness and compassion, he stepped into the realm of purpose—an expansive landscape where his pain could find meaning, where his struggles could become motivation and inspiration toward a brighter tomorrow.

As Ernest closed the chapter, a sense of purpose welled within him, a flame ignited by the understanding that his past did not define him but rather propelled him toward a future filled with purpose and meaning.

With each word etched upon his heart, he pledged to honor his journey by embracing his unique ability to transform pain into purpose—a testament to the resilience of the human spirit.

And so, with the chapter's teachings etched deeply into his soul, Ernest set forth on his path, his heart ablaze with the belief that he had the power to rewrite his story.

In the symphony of life, he would wield his pain as a brush, painting a masterpiece of purpose and inspiration for all who had the privilege to witness his transformative journey.

Chapter 6
Mirror of Self-Discovery

As Ernest gazed into the mirror of truth, he saw the flickering flames of passion and the ashes of missed opportunities. The reflection held the weight of unspoken desires and untapped potential, whispering of the roads not taken and the choices left behind.

His eyes traced the lines etched upon his face, each one telling a story. There were laughter lines, evidence of joyous moments that had lit up his existence. But there were also furrows, etched by worry and regret, reminders of the battles fought within.

Ernest's search for meaning led him deeper into the chapter of self-examination. He delved into the recesses of his soul, unearthing buried memories and forgotten aspirations. He confronted his fears and insecurities, acknowledging the doubts that had haunted him for far too long.

With each layer he peeled back, Ernest discovered hidden strengths and untamed passions. He recognized the power of vulnerability, understanding that it takes courage to confront oneself, to embrace the imperfect, and to acknowledge the wounds that shaped him.

The mirror unveiled his authentic self, stripped of pretense and societal expectations. It revealed a person yearning for growth, a seeker of truth and purpose. Ernest marveled at the complexity within him, the capacity for both darkness and light, for both love and pain.

This journey of self-discovery was not without its challenges. Ernest stumbled upon uncomfortable truths and acknowledged his shortcomings.

Yet, within those revelations lay the seeds of transformation. He understood that self-awareness was the key to unlocking his full potential and living a life aligned with his deepest values.

As Ernest closed the chapter of self-examination, he felt a renewed sense of clarity and purpose. The mirror reflected his true essence, and he embraced it with acceptance and compassion.

He knew that this profound journey was just the beginning—a cornerstone towards a life lived authentically, a life where he could face himself with unwavering honesty and embrace the boundless possibilities that awaited him.

With newfound clarity, Ernest embarked on a path of self-transformation. He recognized that the mirror of truth had revealed not only his flaws but also his potential for growth and change. Armed with this understanding, he set out to nurture the strengths he had discovered within himself and to confront the shadows that had held him back.

Ernest sought out knowledge and wisdom from various

sources. He devoured books that explored the depths of human psychology, spirituality, and personal development.

He sought guidance from mentors and engaged in meaningful conversations with friends who had also embarked on their own journeys of self-discovery.

Through self-reflection and introspection, Ernest began to dismantle the masks he had worn for so long. He let go of the need to please others and embraced his authentic self, understanding that true fulfillment could only come from living in alignment with his values and passions.

He confronted his fears head-on, pushing himself beyond the limits of his comfort zone. He took risks, knowing that growth and self-discovery often reside just beyond the boundaries of familiarity.

With each step forward, Ernest felt a renewed sense of empowerment and liberation, as if he were shedding the weight of expectations that had held him captive.

As Ernest's journey unfolded, he started to make conscious choices that aligned with his true desires. He prioritized self-care and nurtured his physical, mental, and emotional well-being. He surrounded himself with supportive and uplifting individuals who encouraged his growth and shared in his quest for self-realization.

The scars he had once seen as blemishes now became

symbols of resilience and lessons learned. Ernest embraced the lessons from his past, reframing them as God's lessons towards personal growth rather than as hindrances. He forgave himself for perceived mistakes and saw them as opportunities for growth and self-compassion.

Through self-examination, Ernest discovered a sense of purpose that burned brightly within him. He uncovered his unique gifts and talents, recognizing that he had the power to make a positive impact on the world around him. With renewed determination, he set goals aligned with his newfound purpose and took deliberate action to manifest his dreams.

The journey of self-discovery was not without its challenges. Ernest encountered setbacks and faced moments of doubt. However, armed with the knowledge of his own resilience, he pressed forward with unwavering determination.

As Ernest continued to navigate the depths of his being, he embraced the ever-evolving nature of self-discovery. He understood that the journey was not linear but rather a continuous process of growth and self-reflection. He approached each day with an open heart and mind, knowing that within him lay infinite possibilities waiting to be explored.

And so, with courage in his heart and a steadfast commitment to self-examination, Ernest continued forward on his path of self-discovery, eager to unravel the layers of his being, to unearth the truths that would lead him to a life of authenticity, fulfillment, and profound self-understanding.

As Ernest delved deeper into his journey of self-discovery, he began to realize the interconnectedness of his inner world with the outer world. He understood that his personal growth and transformation had a ripple effect, influencing not only his own life but also those around him.

With this newfound awareness, Ernest became intentional about nurturing meaningful connections with others. He engaged in deep, authentic conversations that allowed him to explore different perspectives and learn from diverse experiences.

He sought to understand and empathize with others, recognizing that their journeys of self-discovery were just as intricate and valuable as his own.

Ernest also learned the importance of self-compassion and extending it to others. He realized that everyone he encountered was on their own unique path, and judgment served no purpose in his quest for growth. Instead, he embraced empathy and kindness as guiding principles, supporting others in their own journeys while remaining true to himself.

Throughout his exploration, Ernest discovered the transformative power of gratitude and mindfulness. He cultivated a practice of being present in each moment, savoring the beauty of simple joys and finding solace in the midst of challenges. Gratitude became a compass that guided him, helping him to recognize and appreciate the abundance in his life.

As Ernest continued to traverse the landscapes of self-examination, he realized that self-discovery was not a destination but a lifelong process. He acknowledged that he would continue to evolve, to learn, and to grow, even as he unearthed deeper layers of his being.

This understanding filled him with a sense of excitement and curiosity as he eagerly embraced the unknown and the possibilities it held.

With each passing day, Ernest's journey of self-discovery became an integral part of his existence. It influenced his choices, his relationships, and his contribution to the world.

He recognized that his commitment to self-examination was not self-indulgent but rather an act of service to himself and others, as he sought to create a ripple effect of authenticity, compassion, and personal fulfillment.

And so, with a heart brimming with gratitude and a mind open to the infinite depths of self-discovery, Ernest continued to walk his path with courage and resilience.

He embraced the challenges as opportunities for growth, the setbacks as lessons in resilience, and the triumphs as milestones of his journey.

As the pages of his life turned, Ernest knew that he would encounter new chapters, each beckoning him to explore and embrace the truths within.

With unwavering determination and an unwavering commitment to self-examination, he stepped forward, ready to face whatever lay ahead on his profound journey of self-discovery.

With each step along his profound journey of self-discovery, Ernest became increasingly attuned to the whispers of his inner voice, the guiding compass that led him closer to his authentic self. He learned to trust his intuition, recognizing it as a powerful ally on his path.

Embracing the chapter on self-examination ignited a spark within Ernest—a spark of creativity and self-expression. He realized that by embracing his truest self, he had the ability to tap into a wellspring of inspiration that flowed from deep within his soul.

With renewed passion, he embarked on artistic endeavors that allowed him to channel his emotions and share his unique perspective with the world.

Ernest's journey of self-discovery also led him to explore the beauty and interconnectedness of the natural world. He found solace in the tranquility of forests, the rhythmic crash of ocean waves, and the vibrant colors of a sunset. Nature became his sanctuary, reminding him of the inherent harmony and wisdom that surrounded him.

As he continued his exploration, Ernest encountered moments of profound self-acceptance and forgiveness. He recognized that to embrace his authentic self truly, he needed to release the burden of past mistakes and embrace the imperfections that made him human. Through forgiveness, he found liberation, allowing himself to grow and evolve without being held hostage by regrets.

Ernest's self-examination journey extended beyond himself and into his relationships. He recognized the importance of fostering connections built on authenticity, empathy, and mutual growth.

He surrounded himself with individuals who uplifted him, celebrated his victories, and challenged him to become the best version of himself. Together, they embarked on a shared journey of self-discovery, supporting and inspiring one another along the way.

Through self-examination, Ernest also discovered the power of giving back to his community. He realized that by sharing his newfound insights and experiences, he could help others on their own paths of self-discovery.

Whether through mentoring, volunteering, or simply lending a listening ear, he became a source of inspiration and encouragement for those seeking their own truth.

As Ernest neared the culmination of his self-examination journey, he reflected on the transformative impact it had on his life. He had peeled back the layers of his being, confronted his fears, and embraced his vulnerabilities. In doing so, he had unearthed a reservoir of strength, resilience, and authenticity that would forever guide him.

With gratitude in his heart and a deep sense of purpose, Ernest embarked on the next phase of his journey—a life lived in alignment with his truest self.

The chapter on self-examination would forever remain a cornerstone, reminding him of the courage it took to face his innermost truths and the infinite possibilities that lay before him.

And so, Ernest stepped forward, eager to embrace the chapters yet unwritten, knowing that the journey of self-discovery would continue to unfold as long as he remained open to growth, willing to learn from both the triumphs and the trials that awaited him. With a fearless heart, he embarked on a life of authenticity, self-compassion, and profound self-understanding.

Chapter 7
Writing My Story

In the quiet solitude of his room, Flashes of memories of my grandmother raced through my mind and sparked my heart. My parents' words vibrated within me, resonating with a fervor I had never felt before. A tremor of anticipation coursed through my veins as he contemplated the power of becoming the author of my own life story.

Gone were the days of passively accepting the images and direction others had written for me, the lines I dutifully recited without questioning their authenticity.

No longer would I seek external validation or dance to the tunes of societal expectations. It was time to seize the pen and wield it with purpose.

As I penned Chapter 7, the pages breathed life into my weary spirit. The author's voice within me, a gentle whisper of encouragement, urged me to embrace my inherent creativity and carve his own path.

It was a call to liberation, an invitation to step into the vast canvas of my existence and paint it with vibrant hues. With a determined heart and trembling hands, I picked up my pen. Emotions flowed, and ink-stained the pages like a beautiful sunset on the beach, an elixir of self-expression, as he meticulously crafted the first strokes of my authentic story.

Each word etched upon the parchment carried the weight of my dreams, the echoes of my aspirations, and the fire of my passion.

This book reminded me that I possessed a unique perspective, a kaleidoscope of experiences and emotions that only he could share.

It urged me to embrace his vulnerabilities, to find strength in his flaws, and to weave them into the tapestry of his narrative with unabashed honesty.

Through tears of both sorrow and triumph, I excavated the depths of his being. I unearthed buried dreams, whispered secrets, and dormant desires that had long been stifled by fear.

The book taught me that my story deserved to be heard, cherished, and celebrated, for it was a testimony of his very existence.

With each chapter he penned, Ernest discovered newfound courage. He defied the limitations imposed by doubt and uncertainty, daring to believe in the boundless potential that resided within him.

He infused his story with resilience, tenacity, and an unwavering faith in the power of his own voice.

Facing Ernest Porter

As the emotions flowed, Ernest's soul unfurled like a delicate blossom. He embraced the moments of darkness, tracing their contours with tender strokes, knowing that they had shaped him into the person he had become. He celebrated the triumphs, the small victories that illuminated his journey like stars in a velvety night sky.

The book whispered secrets of self-discovery, guiding me toward the essence of his being. It urged him to embrace the beauty of his imperfections, to find solace in the cracks and crevices that made him whole.

It was in those imperfections that his story gained depth and authenticity, resonating with others who longed to find their own voice.

With each word he penned, Ernest felt a surge of liberation, as if shackles that had bound him for far too long were falling away.

He reveled in the freedom to express his truth, unencumbered by societal expectations or the fear of judgment. His story became a beacon of hope, a testament to the resilience of the human spirit.

As I reached the final paragraph of his chapter, my heart swelled with gratitude. The book had gifted me with the wisdom to shape his own narrative, embrace the power of my voice, and weave a tapestry of authenticity.

I realized that his story was not merely ink on paper but a symphony of emotions and experiences that had the potential to touch lives, inspire, and ignite change.

At that moment, I understood that he was not just authoring his own story. I was becoming a storyteller, a weaver of tales, inviting others to embark on their own journeys of self-discovery and empowerment.

And with that realization, he closed the book, ready to continue his odyssey of self-expression, armed with the unwavering belief that his story mattered.

In the depths of his being, Ernest felt a yearning, a call to reclaim the pen of his life and compose a symphony of authenticity. The book's words resonated with him like a gentle breeze, whispering tales of liberation and self-expression. It was time to shatter the chains of conformity and become the author of his own story.

With each page turned, the ink of possibility coursed through Ernest's veins, awakening a dormant creativity that had long been suppressed. He realized that he had been playing the roles assigned to him by society, bending and contorting himself to fit into their narrow boxes of expectations. But no more!

A surge of determination swelled within him like a mighty river breaking through the barriers of self-doubt. He understood that his worth was not dependent on the opinions of others but rather on the authenticity of his own voice. The time had come to weave his own tapestry of dreams, passions, and aspirations.

Authoring this book reminded Ernest that he possessed the power to shape his narrative to infuse his experiences with purpose and meaning.

He no longer had to be a passive character, swept away by the currents of circumstance. Instead, he could step boldly onto the stage of life, armed with a pen of intention and a heart full of conviction.

Gone were the days of seeking validation from others, of relying on external applause to validate his existence. The true measure of his worth lay within, in the depths of his soul, waiting to be unearthed and celebrated. He embraced the notion that his story was worthy of being told, regardless of its twists and turns.

Oh yes, I understood that writing my own story meant embracing vulnerability, baring his soul on the pages of life. It meant daring to dream beyond the confines of societal norms, unearthing the dormant passions that had been whispered away by fear. Each word he penned was a declaration of self-ownership, a testament to his unique essence.

Ernest wanted this book to urge others to embrace the uncertainties and challenges that lay ahead, for within them were the seeds of growth and transformation.

It reminded him that life was not a linear narrative but a tapestry of experiences woven with joy, sorrow, triumph, and defeat. Every chapter held the potential for a profound lesson or a breathtaking revelation.

When the image of my life story has been inked on life's pages had been penned by the hands of others for far too long. One awaking morning, I grew weary of playing the puppet in someone else's grand production and longed to grasp the quill and write my own symphony of existence.

The book whispered the timeless truth that it was he who held the power to author his destiny, to etch his dreams upon the parchment of reality. As the ink of his pen danced across the blank canvas of his life, I began to witness the magic of self-creation.

He painted with bold strokes of courage, illuminating the darkest corners of his fears. He wove intricate patterns of resilience, threading together the fragments of his past to create a mosaic of strength. With each word etched onto the parchment of his existence, I discovered a newfound freedom, a liberation of his spirit.

I no longer sought approval or validation, for I had embraced the truth that my worthiness was inherent, woven into the very fabric of my being.

The weight of conformity, the burden of societal expectations, had shackled his spirit for far too long. Once, I blindly walked a path paved by the footsteps of others; my voice silenced beneath the clamor of their opinions.

But no more. No more would this man dance to the tunes of others' desires, for I had found the courage to compose his own melody.

With trembling hands and a heart afire, Ernest gripped the quill, its slender form an extension of his own yearning soul. He dipped it into the inkwell of passion, watching as droplets of possibility splattered onto the blank canvas of his life.

The strokes of his pen would no longer be dictated by external forces but by the rhythm of his own heartbeat.

Gone were the days of seeking validation, of molding himself to fit into the narrow molds cast by others. The book's wisdom resonated within him, reminding him that he was a masterpiece in progress, a kaleidoscope of colors waiting to burst forth. His story would be woven with threads of authenticity, unabashedly embracing the unique tapestry of his being.

Ernest's pen danced across the pages, etching words that dripped with his essence. He traced the contours of his dreams, painting vibrant scenes of love, adventure, and growth. The strokes were bold, uninhibited, each letter a testament to his courage to defy convention and embrace the uncharted territories of his own soul.

In the solace of his writing sanctuary, Ernest discovered a sanctuary within himself. It was a sacred space where his dreams took flight, where his aspirations found a home. The symphony of his life story played on, each chapter unfolding with grace and purpose.

Through the valleys of uncertainty and the peaks of triumph, Ernest's story would unfold. The book urged him to unleash the power of his voice, to let his words soar like birds in the vast expanse of possibility. No longer would he hold back the truths etched within his heart, for the world needed to hear the echoes of his experience.

With every word he penned, Ernest discovered a newfound freedom. The shackles of conformity crumbled; their remnants scattered like dust in the wind. He realized that his story was not meant to be censored or watered down but an unapologetic declaration of his existence. In its rawness lay its power, resonating with others who sought their own liberation.

The book's pages whispered secrets of resilience, urging Ernest to persevere when doubt threatened to consume him. It reminded him that setbacks were merely plot twists, opportunities for character development. The hero's journey was not without its trials, but it was through these challenges that he would discover his true strength.

As the ink dried upon the parchment, Ernest marveled at the story he had crafted. It was a testament to his courage, a testament to the power of self-belief.

Facing Ernest Porter

With tears of joy streaming down his face, he closed the book and held it to his chest, knowing that within its words lay the blueprint for his metamorphosis.

The pen had become his sword and his story, an anthem of authenticity. Ernest had found his voice, his purpose, and with each turn of the page, he breathed life into the narrative that would define him.

From that moment forward, he would live not as a character in someone else's tale but as the protagonist of his own grand adventure.

And as Ernest closed the book, a tear of gratitude escaped his eye. He marveled at the transformative power of storytelling, at the ability to shape his destiny with the strokes of his pen.

From that moment on, he vowed to honor his truth, to live authentically, and to continue writing the extraordinary tale of his own life.

And as he set the quill down, a renewed sense of purpose filled his soul. He stepped into the boundless realm of his potential, ready to embrace the unwritten pages that awaited him.

The book had guided him, but now, he was the author of his own destiny, ready to create a masterpiece that would echo in the hearts of generations to come.

Chapter 8
Embracing Self Discovery

As I embarked on the concluding chapter of this book, dedicated to self-healing, personal growth, and continuous progress, I found myself immersing deeper into its pages.

A whirlwind of emotions stirred within me, much like a tempestuous storm, as the words resonated in the profound corners of my soul. They sparked a fire that had long lay dormant, waiting to be awakened.

The journey of self-discovery had now begun, and the persistent call to embrace my inherent worth could no longer ignored.

With each turn of the page, the book unveiled new insights and revelations, like hidden treasures waiting to be discovered. The words danced before my eyes, forming a tapestry of wisdom and inspiration.

They whispered ancient secrets and timeless truths, urging me to shed the layers of doubt and insecurity.

As I delved deeper into expressing a new outlook on life, penning a book on teaching self-values became more important than ever. A profound sense of liberation washes over me. It was as if the weight of past disappointments and self-imposed limitations began to lift, making space for a renewed sense of purpose and potential.

The chapters became gateways to profound introspection, inviting me to confront my fears and embrace the fullness of my being.

Within the pages of this transformative book, I found solace in the knowledge that self-healing was not a linear path but a perpetual motion of growth and evolution. It reminded me that life's challenges were not obstacles but opportunities for inner transformation and resilience.

The words that I authored produced my own inspired guiding light, illuminating the path ahead as I navigated the uncharted territory of self-discovery.

They encouraged me to celebrate my unique gifts and talents, to honor the depths of my emotions, and to cultivate self-compassion in moments of vulnerability.

As I approached the last chapter, I recognized that this book was not merely a collection of words on paper; it was a catalyst for profound change. It had ignited a spark within me, awakening a dormant fire that burned with the determination to rise above limitations and embrace the full spectrum of my worth.

And so, with a mixture of excitement and trepidation, I closed the book and placed it on the table, knowing that it was more than just a book but a redemptive teaching that would forever be imprinted on my heart and aid people around the world in finding their pathway to inner freedom. The journey of self-healing and elevation continued beyond its pages, for I had become an active participant in the narrative of my own life.

Armed with newfound resilience and a deep-seated belief in my worth, I stepped forward into the world, ready to embrace the endless possibilities that awaited me.

No longer bound by self-doubt, I embarked on a path of self-empowerment, guided by the wisdom and lessons learned from the transformative book that had sparked the flame of my soul.

With every step I took, I carried within me the echoes of the book's teachings—reminders of my inherent worth, the resilience of my spirit, and the boundless potential that resided within.

The closing of this chapter marked not an end, but a new beginning—a chapter filled with self-discovery, growth, and the perpetual motion of becoming the best version of myself.

As I ventured beyond the confines of the book's pages, I realized that the journey of self-discovery was an ongoing process, an ever-unfolding story waiting to be unveiled.

The book had served as a catalyst, igniting a flame of inspiration and self-belief within me, but now it was my turn to take the reins and become the author of my own narrative.

Facing Ernest Porter

With each passing day, I embraced the call to embrace my worth more fiercely. I let go of the shackles of self-doubt and stepped into a newfound confidence guided by the lessons I had learned.

I allowed myself to be vulnerable, recognizing that true strength lay in authenticity and self-acceptance.

The journey was not without its challenges. There were moments of doubt and setbacks, but I refused to let them define me.

I drew upon the reservoir of resilience I had discovered within, reminding myself that every stumble was an opportunity for growth and every obstacle was a chance to prove my inner strength.

I sought out new experiences and surrounded myself with uplifting souls who encouraged my journey of self-elevation. I dove into the depths of my passions, exploring avenues that resonated with the essence of my being.

I pursued knowledge, both internal and external, continuously expanding my horizons and pushing the boundaries of what I believed was possible.

In this perpetual motion of self-discovery, I found a profound sense of liberation. I no longer sought validation from external sources, for I had come to understand that my worth emanated from within. I embraced my uniqueness, celebrating the intricacies that made me who I was.

Through self-healing, I unearthed the power of forgiveness, both for myself and others. I released the burdens of past grievances, freeing up space in my heart and mind for love, compassion, and joy.

I discovered the strength in vulnerability, allowing myself to feel deeply and express my emotions authentically.

As the chapters of my life unfolded, I realized that self-discovery was not a destination but a continuous journey. I committed myself to a lifetime of growth, understanding that there would always be new lessons to learn and layers to peel back.

In the end, the book served as a catalyst, a starting point that propelled me onto a path of self-empowerment and fulfillment. I had taken the wisdom it imparted and woven it into the very fabric of my being.

The fire it ignited within me burned brighter than ever, guiding me toward a life filled with purpose, authenticity, and an unwavering belief in my own worth.

And so, I stepped forward into the unknown, ready to embrace whatever lay ahead. The closing of this chapter was not an end but a prelude to the next chapter of my life—one that held infinite possibilities, untapped potential, and the promise of a soul that had embraced its worth and would forever strive for elevation and growth.

Facing Ernest Porter

With each step I took on this journey of self-discovery, the path ahead became clearer, illuminated by the light of my newfound self-worth.

I encountered new challenges and triumphs, each one serving as a testament to my inner strength and resilience.

I embraced the power of self-love, nurturing my mind, body, and spirit with care and compassion. I recognized that my worth was not contingent upon external validation but rooted in my inherent value as a human being.

I let go of comparisons and societal expectations, allowing myself to shine authentically and unapologetically.

As I delved deeper into the realms of personal growth, I discovered the joy of perpetual motion—the exhilarating dance of progress and transformation. I understood that self-improvement was not a destination but a lifelong commitment to becoming the best version of myself.

I sought out mentors and teachers who could guide me on this path, offering wisdom and insights that resonated with my soul. I immersed myself in books, workshops, and meaningful conversations, constantly expanding my knowledge and understanding of the world around me. The flames of my passion burned brighter than ever before.

I pursued my dreams with unwavering determination, embracing the uncertainties and challenges that came along the way. I recognized that failure was not a reflection of my worth but an opportunity to gain experience, grow, and evolve.

In the depths of my being, I discovered a wellspring of creativity waiting to be unleashed. I expressed myself through art, writing, music, and other forms of self-expression.

I tapped into the infinite reservoir of inspiration that flowed through me, allowing my unique voice to be heard.

As I closed the last chapter of this book of self-healing and elevation, I realized that the journey had not truly ended. It had transformed into a lifelong commitment—a commitment to continuous self-discovery, growth, and the perpetual motion of becoming.

With every breath I took, I embraced the call to elevate not only myself but also those around me. I became a beacon of light, inspiring others to embark on their own journey of self-discovery and embrace their inherent worth.

And so, with a heart filled with gratitude and a spirit brimming with determination, I set forth into the vast expanse of possibilities that lay ahead.

The book of self-healing had served its purpose—it had ignited the fire within me, guided me on a path of self-discovery, and reminded me of the boundless potential that resides within us all.

Facing Ernest Porter

As the chapters of my life continued to unfold, I knew that I would face new challenges and embrace new opportunities. I would stumble, but I would rise again. I would question, but I would seek answers. I would fall, but I would always find the strength to stand taller than before.

The journey of self-healing, elevation, and perpetual motion was not just a chapter in a book—it was the essence of my existence, the foundation upon which I built a life of purpose, fulfillment, and unwavering self-belief.

And so, with unwavering determination and a heart filled with infinite possibilities, I stepped forward, ready to embrace the next chapter of my extraordinary journey.

About The Author

In the depths of his heart, Ernest Porter, the author of the remarkable book "Facing Ernest," has ignited a fire that drives him forward, propelling him on a transformative journey. With fervor and unwavering determination, he embarks on a courageous mission to peel back the layers of his existence, eager to reveal himself in a new, radiant light.

Passion courses through Ernest's veins like a river of molten emotions, surging with intensity and purpose. It fuels his every word, every thought, as he reaches deep into the depths of his soul, unearthing the rawest aspects of his being.

With each stroke of his pen, he weaves intricate tapestries of profound vulnerability and profound strength, blending them harmoniously to create a symphony of self-discovery. Ernest's path is not an easy one. It winds through the treacherous landscapes of doubt and fear, threatening to derail his progress.

Yet, his indomitable spirit refuses to yield, for he knows that within the crucible of adversity lies the spark of transformation. He embraces the challenges with open arms, using them as stepping stones to ascend to new heights, forever pushing the boundaries of his own potential.

His words dance across the pages, imbued with the essence

Facing Ernest Porter

of his soul. They resonate with readers, captivating their hearts and stirring their deepest emotions. Ernest's message is one of hope and resilience, a beacon of light in a world shrouded in darkness.

Through his introspection and self-revelation, he implores others to embark on their own quests for authenticity, inviting them to shed their masks and embrace the beauty of their true selves.

As Ernest bares his soul, he becomes a guiding light for those lost in the labyrinth of self-doubt. With profound empathy, he understands the weight of the human experience, and through his artistry, he offers solace and understanding to those who yearn for connection and meaning.

His words, like a gentle embrace, comfort the wounded hearts, inspiring them to heal and grow. Ernest Porter, the author who once penned "Facing Ernest Porter," has now become an embodiment of his own work.

With unwavering passion and unyielding determination, he fearlessly ventures into uncharted territories of self-expression, illuminating the darkest corners of his being. Through his journey, he reminds us of all that within the depths of our souls lies the power to transform, to rise above our limitations, and to shine brilliantly in the world.

With every page turned, Ernest Porter delves deeper into the labyrinth of his emotions, unearthing buried fragments of his soul that have long yearned for recognition. Each word he spills onto the blank canvas is infused with the weight of his experiences, an intimate testament to the joys, the sorrows, and the indelible scars that have shaped his existence.

His mission to reveal himself in a new light is not just an artistic endeavor; it is a profound act of vulnerability, an act that demands the utmost courage. Ernest confronts the ghosts of his past with a steady gaze, refusing to be held captive by their haunting whispers any longer.

Through the power of his words, he lays bare his deepest fears, his hidden dreams, and the delicate intricacies of his humanity. In this journey of self-discovery, Ernest's passion becomes a lifeline, an anchor that keeps him grounded amidst the tempestuous waves of doubt and self-questioning.

It fuels his relentless pursuit of truth, urging him to peel away the layers of pretense and societal expectations, revealing the authentic essence that resides within. Yet, as he unveils his true self, Ernest understands the fragility of his revelations.

He knows that vulnerability, like a tender blossom, a person's passion and identity can easily crushed under the weight of judgment and criticism. Standing in this newness, he refused silence and chose to speak out! With a voice trembling with emotion, he invites the world to witness his transformation, to bear witness to

Facing Ernest Porter

the beauty that emerges when one embraces their true nature. His passion burns like a roaring fire, igniting the souls of others as they encounter his words. Strangers become kindred spirits, connecting through the shared experience of navigating the labyrinth of the human condition.

Through his artistry, Ernest becomes a guide, a mentor, and a companion, offering solace to those who have felt unseen and unheard. In this journey of self-revelation, Ernest Porter lays his emotions bare upon the altar of authenticity.

With trembling hands and a heart laid bare, he allows his vulnerability to become his greatest strength. He inspires others to embark on their own odyssey of self-discovery, to embrace the raw, untamed emotions that reside within, and to find solace in the liberation that comes from embracing one's true self.

As Ernest continues to write, his words reverberate with the weight of a thousand souls. They echo through the corridors of human existence, reminding us of all that we are not alone in our struggles, our hopes, and our dreams.

In the tapestry of his emotions, he weaves a universal story of resilience, reminding us that within our own depths, we possess the power to heal, grow, and emerge as vibrant beings capable of illuminating the world with our unique light.

Ernest Porter, the author who once gazed into the reflection of his soul, now shares that reflection with the world. With unwavering devotion and a heart bursting with emotions, he illuminates the path for others to embark on their own transformative journeys.

In his words, we find solace, inspiration, and the courage to embrace our own authenticity. And through his unwavering passion, he reminds us of all that within the depths of our vulnerability lies the infinite potential for self-discovery, love, and profound connection.

Made in the USA
Middletown, DE
09 July 2024